FARM ANIMALS

Dogs

by Hollie Endres

BLASTOFF! READERS

BELLWETHER MEDIA • MINNEAPOLIS, MN

Note to Librarians, Teachers, and Parents:

Blastoff! Readers are carefully developed by literacy experts and combine standards-based content with developmentally-appropriate text.

Level 1 provides the most support through repetition of high-frequency words, light text, predictable sentence patterns, and strong visual support.

Level 2 offers early readers a bit more challenge through varied simple sentences, increased text load, and less repetition of high frequency words.

Level 3 advances early-fluent readers toward fluency through increased text and concept load, less reliance on visuals, longer sentences, and more literary language.

Level 4 builds reading stamina by providing more text per page, increased use of punctuation, greater variation in sentence patterns, and increasingly challenging vocabulary.

Level 5 encourages children to move from "learning to read" to "reading to learn" by providing even more text, varied writing styles, and less familiar topics.

Whichever book is right for your reader, Blastoff! Readers are the perfect books to build confidence and encourage a love of reading that will last a lifetime!

JB

This edition first published in 2008 by Bellwether Media.

No part of this publication may be reproduced in whole or in part without written permission of the publisher. For information regarding permission, write to Bellwether Media Inc., Attention: Permissions Department, Post Office Box 1C, Minnetonka, MN 55345-9998.

Library of Congress Cataloging-in-Publication Data
Endres, Hollie J.
  Dogs / by Hollie J. Endres.
    p. cm. – (Blastoff! Readers: farm animals)
Summary: "A basic introduction to dogs and how they live on the farm. Simple text and full color photographs. Developed by literacy experts for students in kindergarten through third grade"–Provided by publisher.
  Includes bibliographical references and index.
  ISBN-13: 978-1-60014-083-9 (hardcover : alk. paper)
  ISBN-10: 160014-083-1 (hardcover : alk. paper)
  1. Dogs–Juvenile literature. I. Title.

  SF426.5.E53 2008
  636.7–dc22

Contents

Some dogs live
on farms.
They help farmers.

Dogs **protect** the farm. They watch out for wild animals. A fox may try to eat farm animals.

Dogs use their **sense** of smell to protect the farm. They can smell wild animals nearby.

Dogs use their sense of hearing. They **perk** up their ears to listen for wild animals.

11

Dogs bark
to scare away
wild animals.

Some dogs **herd**
farm animals.
This dog herds
sheep into a pen.

This dog herds
a **flock** of ducks.

Dogs can
learn to follow
commands
like "**fetch**."

Dogs can work
and play on
the farm.

Glossary

commands—orders given to do something

fetch—to go after and bring back an object

flock—a group of birds

herd—to gather or lead animals together in a group

perk—to lift quickly

protect—to guard and keep away anything that would cause harm

sense—the way a person or animal learns something through their body; the five senses are hearing, smell, sight, touch, and taste.

To Learn More

AT THE LIBRARY

Brown, Ken. *Mucky Pup.* New York: Dutton, 1997.

Dalgeish, Sharon. *Working Dogs.* New York: Chelsea Clubhouse, 2005.

Schuh, Mari C. *Dogs on the Farm.* Mankato, Minn.: Capstone Press, 2002.

ON THE WEB

Learning more about farm animals is as easy as 1, 2, 3.

1. Go to www.factsurfer.com

2. Enter "farm animals" into search box.

3. Click the "Surf" button and you will see a list of related web sites.

With factsurfer.com, finding more information is just a click away.

Index

The photographs in this book are reproduced through the courtesy of: Eric Isselee, front cover; Per Magnus Persson/Getty Images, p. 5; Jack Cronkhite, p. 7; Theresa Martinez, p. 9; Aleksander Bochenek, p. 11; tbkmedia.de/Alamy, p. 13; Kate Leigh, p. 15; Nick McGowan-Lowe/Alamy, p.17; Karla Caspari, p. 19; Adamsmith/Getty Images, p. 21.